My Bermuda ABC

by Dana Cooper

With thanks to my mother and father.

A a is for Anchor, Angelfish, Aloe plant, Avocado and Allspice trees, Albuoy's Point and Annie's Bay. There is Fort Albert, Agar's Island, the Agricultural Show and the Atlantic Ocean which surrounds Bermuda.

Bb is for Boat, Buoy, Bluebirds,
Banana and Bay Grape trees, Buttery, Boxing
Day, Brain coral, Barracuda, the Bartram, Boaz,
Banjo and Beta Islands, Bob's Valley Lane
and the Birdcage in Hamilton from which
the Bobbies direct traffic.

Cc is for Conch shell, Cahow, Cedar trees and Citrus such as grapefruit, oranges, limes, tangelos and lemons. There are the Cobbler, Castle and Cat Islands, Calypso music, Cricket, Church Street, Cavello Bay, the Carriage Museum and Cassava pie, a tradition at Christmas.

Dd is for Damsel and Doctor fish, Dolphins, Daddy Longleg spiders, Dinghy, Dockyard, the Devonshire Marsh, and Dolly's Bay. There are Dunscombe Rocks, Dock Hill, Dundonald Street and the Delta, Darrell's and Daniel's Islands.

E e is for Easter Lily, Ewing Street,
Echo Lane, Ely's Harbour, Emily's Bay, Elbow Beach,
East End Wharf, Eta Island and Emerald Cross,
a famous piece of treasure found in one of the Spanish
shipwrecks scattered at the bottom of the ocean.

Ff

is for Flying fish, Fishing and Fish pots,
Feather jig, Freesia Flower, Frangipani tree, Forts,
Firefly Reserve, Fagan's Alley, Flatts Bridge,
the Fern and Five Star Islands and Front Street,
which runs along the waterfront in Hamilton.

G g

is for Gaff rig, Gates Fort, Government House, Gibbs Hill Lighthouse, the Grace, Goat and Goose Islands and Gombeys who come out to dance on special holidays.

H h is for Hurricane, Horse and buggy, Hibiscus flower, Harrington Sound, and Hunter's Wharf. There are the Haggis, Hinson and Hen Islands, Horseshoe Beach, the capital of Hamilton, and Hog Money which was the first currency used in Bermuda.

is for Indigo hamlet fish, Ixora plant, Ingham's Fort, the Idol, the Ireland and Iota Islands, Imperial Airways, the first to service Bermuda, and Indian Banyan tree with its twisting roots and branches.

J j

is for Joell's Alley, Jubilee Road,
and all sorts of fish, such as Jumping
Jacks, Jelly and Jewel. There is John Smith's Bay,
Jobson's Cove, and Juan De Bermudez, the Spaniard
after whom Bermuda was named.

K k is for Killick anchor made with rope tied around a heavy stone, Kiskadee bird, Kite, King Square, Knapton Hill, Kappa Island, and the Keepyard at the Maritime Museum where the Royal Navy stored war supplies.

L is for Lizards, Lobsters, Loquat trees, and the Longtail seabird. There are the Little Crumb and Lambda Islands, Leamington Caves, Fort Langton, Lovers Lane and Limestone from which Bermuda houses are made.

is for the Moon,
Mussels, Mangroves, and Monarch butterflies
which depend on Milkweed for food.
There is Moray eel, Moongate, Marine
slip, Mill Creek, My Lord's Bay
and Marshall's Island.

Nn is for Nautical charts, Nurse shark, North Shore Road, Nea Alley, Natural Arches, The Narrows and the Nonsuch and Nelly Islands.

is for Ocean, Octopus, Olivewood tree, Orchard, and Bermuda Onions, known all over the world. There is Old Slip Lane, Orange Valley Road, Ordnance and One Tree Islands, and the Old Opera House which once existed.

P

is for Parrot fish and Portuguese
Man-of-War with its stinging tentacles.
There are the Pawpaw and Palmetto trees, Pearl
Island, the Perfume Factory, and the nine Parishes:
Sandys, Southampton, Warwick, Paget, Pembroke,
Devonshire, Smith's, Hamilton and St. George's.

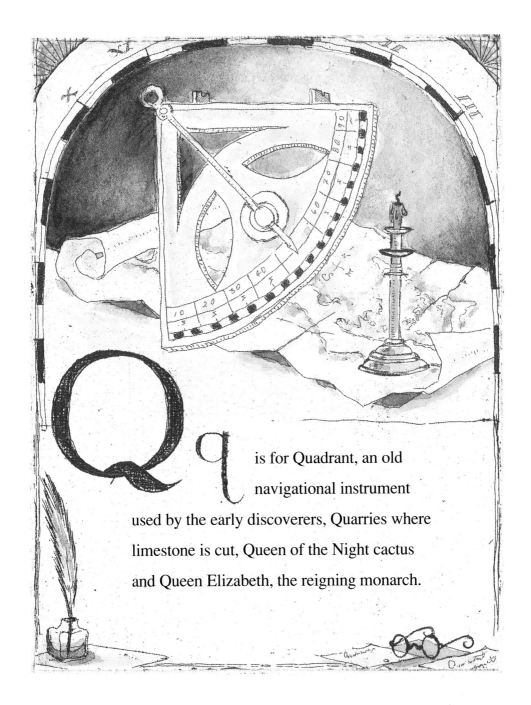

Qq is for Quadrant, an old navigational instrument used by the early discoverers, Quarries where limestone is cut, Queen of the Night cactus and Queen Elizabeth, the reigning monarch.

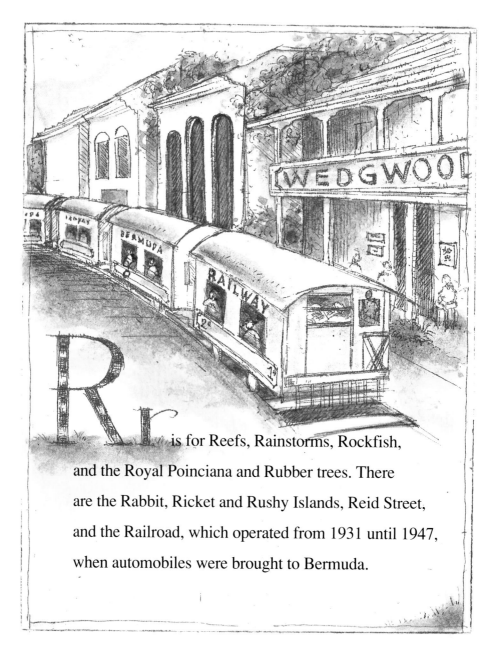

is for Reefs, Rainstorms, Rockfish,
and the Royal Poinciana and Rubber trees. There
are the Rabbit, Ricket and Rushy Islands, Reid Street,
and the Railroad, which operated from 1931 until 1947,
when automobiles were brought to Bermuda.

S s is for the Sun and Stars in the Sky,
Shells from the Sea, Seaweed and Sand. There are
Squirrel fish, Steel drums, Sinky and Shelly Bays,
Saltus Island, Spittal Pond, Shark Oil, still used by
some as a weather indicator, and Sir George Somers,
who was shipwrecked here in 1609.

T is for Tiny Treefrogs whistling "bleep bleep" at night and swimming Turtles. There are the Theta and Tilley Islands, the Tucker Museum, Tobacco Bay, Two Rock Passage and Tea in the afternoon.

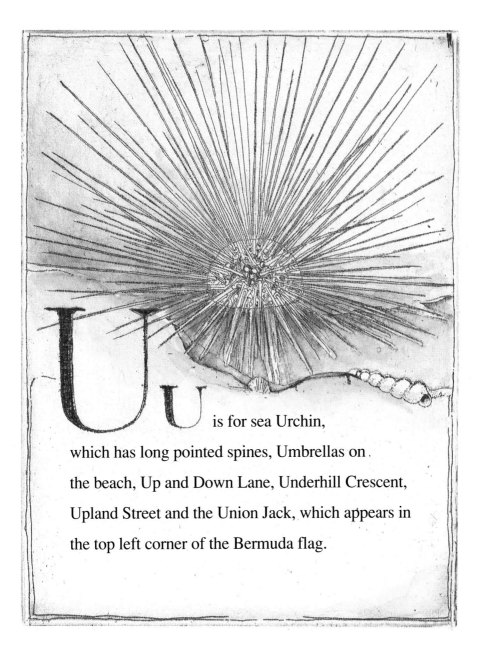

U_u is for sea Urchin,
which has long pointed spines, Umbrellas on
the beach, Up and Down Lane, Underhill Crescent,
Upland Street and the Union Jack, which appears in
the top left corner of the Bermuda flag.

Vv is for Vegetable stands along the side of the road, Verdmont Museum, Valley View Lane, Vickers Bay, Victoria Street, Vines such as the Morning Glory, and Volcano, which is how Bermuda came to be.

Ww is for the Wind, Weathervane, Wahoo, Whip ray, and Walsingham, where Irish Tom Moore wrote poetry. There is the Whitney School, Whalebone Bay, the Watling, White's and Watford Islands and Whales, which can be sighted from land in early spring.

X x is for Xanthium flower

and Xanthidae, which are common mud crabs

found along the shores.

Y is for Yellowtail fish, Yucca plant,

the Yellow-wood and Yew trees,

York Street, Yellow-Crowned Night heron,

Yawning Rock and Yachts, which dot the bays

and harbours throughout the year.

Z z is for Zig Zag

scallop, Zoysia grass, Zuill's Park, Zeta

Island and Zulu, a weather alert which means

the hurricane has passed and presents no

further threat.